How to Be a Contemplative

How to Be a Contemplative

Poems and Brief Reflections by

Judith Valente

© 2025 Judith Valente. All rights reserved.
This material may not be reproduced in any form, published,
reprinted, recorded, performed, broadcast,
rewritten or redistributed without
the explicit permission of Judith Valente.
All such actions are strictly prohibited by law.

Cover design by Shay Culligan
Cover image by J. Alden Marlatt
Author photo by Carleigh Gray

ISBN: 978-1-63980-725-3
Library of Congress Control Number: 2025936133

Kelsay Books
502 South 1040 East, A-119
American Fork, Utah 84003
Kelsaybooks.com

As always, for Charley

Acknowledgments

Grateful acknowledgment is extended to the editors of the following publications in which versions of these poems previously appeared.

After Hours: "Encountering Silence" (Honorable Mention, Mary Blinn Poetry Prize)
Cresset: "Super Wolf Moon"
The Merton Seasonal: "At Thomas Merton's Hermitage on His Death Anniversary"
Parabola: "Vesper Time" (Honorable Mention, Thomas Merton Poetry of the Sacred Contest)
Pavan: "How to Be a Contemplative"
Presence: "After Listening to Composer Arvo Pärt Accept an Honorary Degree," "A Place Called Trouble," "Chemotherapy"
U.S. Catholic: "Lauds," "For Theodore, One Day Old," "Produce Aisle," "River's Thaw," "My Father's Down Vest," "Blessing"

Praise for *How to Be a Contemplative*

Take off your glasses to read Judith Valente's poems in *How To Be A Contemplative*. They will provide insufficient focus. Your naked eye will need to move quickly to see with both microscopic and telescopic vision at only a moment's notice—move from imagining the chambers of the heart and regions of the brain to envisioning "300 billion galaxies." At the same time, you will be called to see the middle-ground as well—the easily visible effects of disturbances of these—the "blinking monitor" measuring a husband's pulse, the diminished flesh consumed by "hungry bones" after chemotherapy, a spacecraft "hurtling toward Jupiter to pierce its inner core." This book reminds us that to "see" the world, we must contemplate it with our inner eye; we must "kneel in wonder at the sight / of a cell's inner workings." Readers will look at the world, indeed the universe, differently after reading Valente's poems. For that, I will be forever grateful.

—Mary Ann B. Miller, founding editor, *Presence Journal,* professor of English, Caldwell University

This book delivers no instructions, except by exemplifying what contemplative art is. These rich and mature lines nudge you into an interior space where the world around you speaks with enhanced intimacy.

—Paul Quenon, OCSO, author of *In Praise of the Useless Life: A Monk's Memoir; A Matter of the Heart: A Monk's Journal; Bells of the Hours, Afternoons with Emily* and *Amounting to Nothing*

Contents

Foreword	17
Prologue	21

PART I

Becoming a Writer	24
For Theodore, One Day Old	26
Super Wolf Moon	28
Lauds	30
After Listening to Composer Arvo Pärt Accept an Honorary Degree	32
Vesper Time	34
Encountering Silence	36
Prayer for 3 a.m.	38
How to Be a Contemplative	40

PART II

At Home	44
Ferragosto	46
Living Beside Dachau	48
Litany	50
English Mass, St. Boniface Church, Munich	52
At Thomas Merton's Hermitage on His Death Anniversary	54
A Place Called Trouble	56
Vine Growing Out of Stone Hermitage, Mount Maiella, Italy	58
Summer of 2022	60
What Peace Is	62

PART III

Haibun for Point Reyes Peninsula	66
Anatomy	70
Chemotherapy	72
Produce Aisle	74
To Joy	76
To Wonder	78
The Almost, But Not Yet	80
River's Thaw	82
My Father's Down Vest	84
Blessing	86

*Sometimes I need only to stand where I am
to be blessed.*
—Mary Oliver, *Evidence*

*Here is an unspeakable secret:
paradise is all around us
and we do not understand.*
—Thomas Merton, *Conjectures of a Guilty Bystander*

Foreword

My ongoing conversation with poet, journalist, and author Judith Valente began with being interviewed by her for the national PBS series, Religion and Ethics Newsweekly. I recall being moved and touched by the depth of insight present in every question and in her personal understanding of how my own art form was grounded in contemplative spirituality and the exploration of finding and experiencing the Sacred in ordinary moments.

I immediately picked up her luminous memoir, *Atchison Blue: A Search for Silence, a Spiritual Home and a Living Fatih* followed by *The Art of Pausing* and *How to Be*. I have continued to look to Judith Valente's writing and witness in the world as a well of deep wisdom and a personal touchstone for being in communion with silence, sound, spiritual home, and living faith.

One of the things I confided to Judith during that first PBS interview was my experience with how artists who write from a grounding in a spiritual tradition are often commercially expected to create using a limited box of eight theological crayons. Don't get me wrong, there have been many beautiful and stirring works created using that specific theological palette. Yet personally, as a Quaker, ardent spiritual seeker, musician, performer, songwriter, poet, and podcast host, I'm a 64-box kind of writer and I let Judith know how deeply I appreciated her sense of nuance, her humility, and the joyous curiosity in her approach to art, faith, and journalism.

Judith's journalistic works, essays, poetry, and retreat leadership are grounded in love of the contemplative life, with a willingness to claim the timeless radical love expressed in the Gospels, but always with a deep and abiding respect for the journey of faith across spiritual tradition, with an eye for the awe and holy presence found in daily things and always with an openness to the transformative experience of mystery. She appreciates and loves what can be found within those eight crayons, but also honors a full rainbow of transformative spiritual experience and thought. In other words, from the start I felt a deep kinship with Judith Valente's work and have continued to look forward to each new offering.

In her newest collection of poetry, *How to Be a Contemplative,* Judith returns to her exploration of encountering the Sacred in what at first appears to be absolutely ordinary moments and things. Whether she's seeing "a post-modern Elijah" in a "dreadlock-sporting newspaper deliverer," or a kind of unadorned miracle found in ten-grain bread with blueberry yogurt on the side in the poem "Blessing," or describing awe in a cherry tree's velvety umbrella of blossoms in the poem "Wonder," she keeps giving us glimpses of an ever-present invisible grace always found just below the surface of daily visible things.

Still, Judith's world of wonder is not all gossamer and sweetness as she describes being a gentle witness and supportive presence when a friend confides that "dying is strenuous work" and asks her to remember that living is "a dream job," or when honoring the moment when she hears a hospital intercom play Brahms' lullaby to announce the birth of a new child only moments after the same intercom announced a code blue indicating the passing of one life into the next mystery.

The picture Judith paints is one that acknowledges the bewildering messiness of being human as she wrestles with the presence of violence and suffering in our world, while still affirming a "mercy within mercy within mercy." I particularly appreciated how in the title poem, "How to Be a Contemplative," Judith doesn't give us pat answers to the question of how we all might live a more present life, but instead humbly suggests "find a window and sit by it" to "take more time and cover less ground" and to practice paying attention, open to what we might find in that singular space, because it is only when we take the time to listen do we open up the possibility of hearing "the voice that calls you by name, that calls you Beloved."

I was honored to be invited to write this foreword to *How to Be a Contemplative,* and am excited for you, dear reader, as you turn the page and personally experience the loveliness and deep wisdom contained in this new collection.

Carrie Newcomer
Bloomington, IN

Carrie Newcomer is an Emmy-winning performer, Grammy-recognized recording artist, and a Top-Ten music writer on the popular Substack platform. She has released 20 albums, including most recently A Great Wild Mercy. *She is the author of three books of poetry and essays, including* Until Now: New Poems *and* A Permeable Life: Poems and Essays. *In recent years she has joined with beloved author Parker J. Palmer on several projects including "The Growing Edge" podcast. She is a recipient of The Shalem Institute's Contemplative Voices Award.*

Prologue

In his beautiful poem "Poetry," Pablo Neruda writes of how poetry "arrived" in search of him. He doesn't know how or where it came from, whether "from winter or a river." Somehow, though, he was summoned, and poetry "touched" him.

If we are lucky in life, poetry will find us, summon us out of the husk of all that is familiar, and launch us on a journey of discovery. Perhaps you can remember the first time a poem "touched" you, spoke to you personally. Each of us carries within us a seed of loneliness, usually planted early in life. Poems are the hands that reach out to us, place an arm around the shoulder in moments of bottomless sorrow and inscrutable happiness.

I like to think of poems as what the ancient Celts called *an anam cara,* a soul friend. Like a soul friend, the words of a well-loved poem—a poem that is taken into the heart—will return to us just when we need to hear those words again. It is a friendship that never expires no matter the distance or the amount of time that passes.

Poems have been my companions since childhood. Not because anyone read poetry to me when I was a young—I didn't grow up in that kind of household—but because the universe of words seemed to me, even at an early age, a good way of making sense of an inscrutable world. To this day, I write to understand my life. I write because I love my life.

Poems are our resistance against aloneness. For what is a poem if not a conversation between two people—an act of compassion that reflects the very roots of the word: *cum passio,* to experience with, to endure with.

For many years now, I've tried to live in a more contemplative, reflective, and intentional manner. I've spent many hours in monasteries across the world. Those experiences helped me to see the sacredness of washing dishes, sweeping a floor, eating breakfast, reading the newspaper, sitting at a dying person's bedside, looking at the moon, or even enduring a sleepless night.

Some poems in this collection, like "What Peace Is," "Litany," and "A Place Called Trouble," emerge directly from the news, sparked perhaps by the many years I spent as a print and broadcast journalist. Others, like "Encountering Silence," "Lauds," and the title poem, "How to Be a Contemplative," reflect the continuous work of seeking the transcendent in the ordinary.

Still other poems, such as "At Home," "Haibun for Point Reyes Peninsula," and "English Mass, St. Boniface Church, Munich," unfolded during travel, when new surroundings and encounters heighten the senses. Some, like "Vine Growing Out of Stone Hermitage," arrived as pure gift.

I have included short reflections to go with each poem, not to "explain" the poem, but to add some soil for further meditation. Every poem is its own specific world. Yet it is my hope that by traveling with me to the worlds contained in each of these poems, you will see the narrative of your own life, and love even more the life you have.

Judith Valente
Normal, IL

PART I

Becoming a Writer

Picture a wooden seat the size of a suitcase in a backyard in northern New Jersey.

Above it, the fan-like leaves of a fig tree, their fine hairs.

Picture the tree's small fruits dangling like teardrops poised at any moment to drop.

Then place a ten-year-old child in that spot overlooking the cross-stitches of the Jersey Central Railroad flowing on their way to anywhere and nowhere.

Let the child look up at the neighbor's clothesline strung like electric wire, at the empty-bodied clothes:

the work shirts, baby pajamas, stained white socks, woman's nightgown thinned from too much washing.

Let her listen for the train's whistle, the rumbling of cars over a distant bridge, a life beyond.

Let her fill each piece of clothing with a story.

This is how it begins. This is how it happens on a summer afternoon.

She notes the tar scent in the air, the shape of grass beneath the rubber soles of her shoes, and how the children playing in a nearby alley screech like cats in the night.

She is soaring above the fig tree, writing words with air, tethered to dry ground but walking in space.

For Reflection:

There comes a moment in every life when we receive an intimation of what we are meant to be and do. As Mary Oliver writes in her poem, "The Journey": *One day you finally knew / what you had to do, and began.* For some of us, if we are lucky, that moment comes at an early age, perhaps as a small child seated on a block of wood beneath a fig tree. Perhaps what sparks it is something as simple as looking up at the neighbors' clothesline. For others the moment might come later in life. What matters is that when the message comes, we listen.

For Theodore, One Day Old

He has traveled so far, he must sleep now
the profound sleep of the laborer.

Fluorescent lights dangle like white monsters.
Slowly his universe magnifies

to four green walls, wool blanket, wicker bassinet.
Thrust from the thrum of the dark world

he hears sounds deep as drums:
voices he will one day claim as his own.

Theós dōros. Te adoro. Dios de oro.

Prayer for the gift of God.
Prayer to the God of golden chances.

The newly-voiced soul stirs in the unfused crown,
elsewhere spent souls rise like mites of dust,

descend into sanitized corners, cluster then disappear.
In a metal cabinet, desire waits. Despair. Death too.

The moon face of the wall clock tick-tocks the minutes,
his chest draws in another 44 newborn breaths.

Pocketful of flesh, he moves like an amphibian, gropes
by touch, by scent. Trawls for what sustains him, sustains us all.

For Reflection:

I wish our memories could reach back to our time in the womb, or at least to those first days after birth when we are becoming acquainted with our strange new world. How amazing—and perhaps disconcerting—those surroundings would seem. Try to imagine the earliest moments of your life, the sights, the sounds, the scents, what you could touch. Then try to reconstruct those moments from the perspective of knowing what lies ahead for you. What if we tried every day to view the routine things in our lives with the unprejudiced eyes of an infant?

Super Wolf Moon

I too must be happy with all around me.
—Li Po

It rises, a white bloodless eye,
egg cupped in the womb of night.
Mover of moods and tides,
fraternal twin of the cold unheeding earth.

What loneliness presses the moon onward,
faithful each night as a monk at Compline?

Or is it the hard determination
of one who's lived too long without sound,
yearning for touch: one more small step,
one more shadow dance upon the chest?

Lone cloud, like an exhaled breath,
passes before its open wolf mouth.

Think of poor Li Po
seeing the moon's reflection
in a wine cup, mistaking its face
for his drinking companion.

Still he sings
alone in the silence, dances with his silhouette,
a friend of moon and shadow
in the time of happiness.

For Reflection:

One way to feel a part of something vaster than ourselves is to step outside each night and gaze at the moon, the stars, and the visible planets. The moon in particular has fascinated Japanese haiku writers over the centuries as well as the Chinese poet Li Po of the 8th century Tang Dynasty, whose work was an inspiration for this poem. The moon speaks of cycles, of the inevitable ebb and flow of life. Have you ever looked at the moon and felt it was speaking to you personally? Imagine the secrets it wishes to impart.

Lauds

Cicadas' hiss and wind's sizzle repeat, repeat: wake up.

Morning's empty glass fills with ghost sounds and scents:

tang of a mower's diesel fuel, clang of bells lolling in a stone tower.

The cypress branches nod, sign to one another in a private language.

Take silence from language. Only dry leaves remain.

A black butterfly alights on my knee,

some old soul in a new coat.

I ask the day for its one word, and it gives it to me:

Enough.

The sleeping dachshund at the foot of my chair stirs, looks up:

the only possible response.

For Reflection:

If we simply sit still long enough in silence, the sights, scents, and sounds that surround us become more intense. They will come to seem like prayer. In most monasteries, the day begins near dawn with prayers known as Lauds, which means praise. It is an act of faith to start the day with gratitude and praise when we don't yet know what will transpire. We come with open hands, expecting there will be good, there will be grace. There are moments, too, when spoken prayer isn't necessary. Our prayer is to look, listen, be quiet, and simply be. It is enough.

After Listening to Composer Arvo Pärt Accept an Honorary Degree

One must purify the soul until it begins to sound.
—Arvo Pärt, speaking at Estonia's St. Vladimir Seminary, 2014

One must purify the soul
the way I wash this white sweater,

my hands roiling the fabric,
wringing the dark stains of my collective failings.

One must purify the soul
the way cold rinses the night air clean

of fog, of mist, and the way moonlight
whitens the January ground.

One must purify the soul resting on one's knees:
also walking along a tree-lined path,

treading slowly on a bed of leaves
before the trees have shed their final questions,

or the way a composer taps a carillon's
bronze bells, seeking one pure note.

One must purify the soul with the antibodies
of failure, with the arnica of humility,

making of the soul the most sensitive instrument,
an instrument of lamentation and light.

For Reflection:

Listening to a musical piece by Arvo Pärt, I sometimes feel as though my soul is rising outside of my body. I was intrigued by Pärt's comparing listening to music to a kind of purification of the soul. There are many far more perfect ways to try to accomplish a kind of interior cleansing than those I list in the poem. Yet, the composer seems to be saying, all we really need to do to achieve a kind of detoxification, is to be still and listen.

Vesper Time

This is how I learned to love:
watching an aging couple
climb the twenty-five stairs
from Spoleto's new quarter
to the old, even on a day
so hot a dropped egg
fried on the stone steps.
Every afternoon at five,
they arrived at the *gelateria,*
he nearly blind, she guiding
him by the arm. They ordered
one scoop between them,
some days *nocciola,* others
pistacchio or *amarena.*
Always at the same table
she would dip a plastic
spoon in the paper cup
and he would open his lips,
receive her offering
like a communion wafer.
Then they headed home
the way they came,
to the house I imagined:
painted espresso cups
lace doilies on sofa arms,
framed image of Santa Rita
di Cascia staring from a wall.
Another afternoon adrift
in their calendar of graces.

For Reflection:

Sometimes we glimpse a sight, perhaps out of the corner of our eye, that leaves a lasting impression. I spotted this elderly Italian couple on an extended stay one year in Spoleto, Italy. I watched them each day perform this afternoon ritual and knew somehow that seeing them had changed something inside of me, though I couldn't name what it was. I tried to write a poem about it, but the words didn't come together. Several years later, after I'd been married for a while myself, the first line of the poem came to me. I had learned from this husband and wife something essential about how to love—simply, routinely, without fanfare.

Encountering Silence

It is in the wordless ceiling beams
overflowing with presence
and the beadlike seeds of the holly oak
that crack open to reveal the wisdom of patience.

In its embrace, all is waking,
even the soap dish, tea cup, and porch steps are expectant.
The boundary blurs between the possible
and what just yesterday seemed lost.

In its embrace, the purple iris finds the courage
to drift open, a lone dandelion breaks free
from the stone pavement, and blades of grass spread like prayer
    flags.
A soundless chant drums in the cave of the heart,

a singular music:
it is not in the bird's song, but in the bird's hushed flight,
not in the wind, but in the still, spring air that beckons,
becomes a kind stranger who walks silently beside us.

For Reflection:

In 1 Kings in Scripture, the prophet Elijah strains to hear the voice of God, first in an earthquake, then in the wind, and then in fire. But the voice isn't in any of those things. Finally, Elijah hears a still, small voice, barely a whisper. On my first night alone in an unfamiliar apartment during an extended stay in Italy, I turned out the lights, crept into bed, and experienced a profound sense of silence. It seemed as though all of the objects around me, from the wooden ceiling beams to the porcelain soap dish, were all speaking to me in the silence. Like Elijah, I no longer felt alone. Perhaps you have had a similarly intense encounter with silence. That kind of experience has never happened to me again.

Prayer for 3 a.m.

Lord, save me from the darkness,
    from the black milk that brittles bones,
        withers flesh

Spare me the answers without questions
    that dart behind my eyes,
        a pack of frightened hares

Let the scent of night earth comfort me,
    along with the mycorrhiza tangled as worms,
        speaking in tree root whispers

Give me sure steps on barefoot carpet,
    let me read the braille of each wall,
        tread swiftly as a ghost

I need the stars to be my silver compass,
    the moon's silent watch,
        the outstretched hand of a porch light

Let the window shades rise,
    quiet each floorboard and mute the wind.
        Let me listen to the music of my breath

until the crows reawaken,
    dawn cracks this black veil,
        and like a long laborer, I rest

For Reflection:

Writing poetry is often a way to work through situations that are perplexing. Throughout my life, I've struggled with insomnia. Sometimes I can't get to sleep until the first cracks of dawn begin spreading through the bedroom window. In this poem, all is backward. I sleep in the light; in darkness I remain awake. Sometimes the world seems to be operating counter to conventional wisdom and patterns, as in a dream. We have to go with it and not fight it, until like an exhausted laborer, we can rest.

How to Be a Contemplative

Find a window. Sit by it.

Stare at the flower box of cosmos,
the bees that kiss the blooms and move on.

Sit, not for just two minutes,
but linger there. Waste time.

Forget the laundry, the grocery list,
the buzzing phone, the writing that waits.

Imagine sitting on a shoreline
listening to the endless rumor of the sea.

Imagine rising and falling like the tide.

Our mistakes are doors, our successes
melt quickly on the tongue.

The face you soon will see in the mirror
is the face of every person you've ever met.

It opens like a book of singular stories
unfolding, encompassing everything:

the bee stings, birdsong, night sweats,
sunrises, sunsets, discoveries, losses.

All of it good, all of it a placeholder for meaning.

Then listen for the one word you yearn to hear,
the voice that calls you by name, that calls you Beloved.

For Reflection:

Wendell Berry's poem "How to Be a Poet" is one I have long admired. I often begin with it at poetry writing workshops. For many years now, I've been a student of the contemplative way of life, having spent considerable time in Benedictine, Trappist, and Camaldolese monasteries where prayer is the main form of activity and silence the preferred language. I've learned that living a more contemplative life doesn't consist of grand gestures or some dramatic experience of instant conversion. It is a slow process of repeated, small daily steps that ultimately marks the soul, like water etching into stone. The poem is not so much a prescription as an intimation of how to be. What lines would you add if asked how to be a contemplative?

PART II

At Home

The woman who owns the weary-looking pizzeria
sometimes sings in the piazza, bursts with a dialect

I don't understand, her thick black hair
streaming behind her. She has few reasons to sing:

husband dead at a young age, raising two young daughters,
and only the same old men come as customers.

This morning at La Madonna del Carmine,
Dom Erminio tells the usual half-dozen regulars

to keep doing good even if their efforts seem like a droplet.
We are both the drop and the ocean, Dom Erminio says.

In late afternoon, the children run out of the *scuola elementare*
waving their construction paper drawings at parents

and grandparents who wait to hug them beside parked cars
as though all the children in the world could be so loved.

I know it's not true. Sometimes I walk among the holly oaks
in the piazza, collect seeds that look like wooden beads,

arrange them in patterns on my bookshelves. Sometimes it feels
as though I am moving through a dream, like the one last night

where I was dancing on a Broadway stage. My partner lifted me,
swung me around and we twirled in the air.

The church bells sound the hours, remind me this is my life:
silent Maiella, its slopes of pines standing at attention,

the sweet-smelling sheets flapping over balcony railings,
and the flatbed truck that sputters up a hill as its driver Vincenzo

shouts into a loudspeaker: *carciofi, mandarini, peperoni, patate.*
My neighbors appear from behind faded doors, they wave

and call to me *Buondì!* They welcome me home.

For Reflection:

Home is a defining character in our lives. We might leave the home we grew up in, but it never truly leaves us. If we are fortunate, though, we can forge another home in a place of our choosing. Then there are the temporary homes we create for ourselves, say, when living for a specific period of time in foreign country. Those stays aren't about how many sites we can take in, but about building relationships, getting to know the intimate rhythms of life in a particular place. This poem arose out of a three-month period in which I lived in Italy, one of the happiest times in my life. Still, as much as I felt a part of my new surroundings, my subconscious let me know in dreams that I still belonged in a strong way to another place as well, the place of my birth. Fortunately, the church bells were there to remind me that we can indeed have more than one place where we belong, where we are home.

Ferragosto

On August 15, 2019, two brothers, ages seven and nine, drowned in the Adriatic Sea on the Feast of the Assumption, a holiday known in Italy as Ferragosto.

We thought the water was a blanket we could throw over our heads
and pull down again, the sea a bed we could rise from.

It was the Feast of the Assumption when Mary enters
paradise, her body assumed whole, uncorrupted.

The hungry sea consumed my brother and me,
fickle in its calm demeanor. We held each other's hands,

tumbled into the water's salty mouth. At first, it was exciting,
the way our father sometimes rolled us over in his arms.

We became fish caught in the rocks' toothy jaws
until we separated into a silent blindness.

I remembered running between trees, how a soccer ball feels,
the scent of my mother's skin, the touch of my father's rough
    hands.

I surrendered to the wordless, undulating movement.
Soon my brother and I were floating above the beach,

women we did not know clasped hands to their mouths,
tears ran down their tanned faces,

men I did not recognize made the sign of the cross.
Our father held our mother as she bowed and moaned.

A pair of white gulls left Y-shaped prints on the sand.
Then I was alone. Then the birds grew silent.

For Reflection:

Ferragosto in Italy falls on August 15th, the Feast of the Assumption. The name means August holiday and it is an important vacation day when just about everyone in the country rides a train or bus to visit family, heads for the beach or mountains, or else goes on a picnic with friends in a local park. My first Ferragosto in Italy is a day I'll never forget. It ended in a tragedy that unfolded in real time for all who were there to witness it. A heavy undertow that day swept away a Chinese immigrant father and his two young sons who were swimming with him in the Adriatic. Lifeguards managed to rescue the father, but after an hours' long search, the boys were found drowned. I felt I couldn't simply go on as though I hadn't witnessed this heartbreak. These boys deserved to be remembered. The poem, in the voice of one of the drowned brothers, is an attempt to speak for them. One of the great gifts of poetry is that it can give a voice to those who can no longer speak for themselves.

Living Beside Dachau

We eat our *spaetzle* salted with ash.
When the chimneys smoke in the distance,
we bake only bread.
Mornings, read Luther's Bible,
evenings, a little Goethe:
every day, read a poem,
sing a song, and speak
a few reasonable words.
Trains roll past, shake
Hummels in the china cabinet.
We shade our lamps with lace,
play Mozart's *Requiem* on the Victrola
and sweep our stone steps
clean of human dust.
Arbeit macht frei:
work makes us free.

For Reflection:

The horror of the ovens and the immense suffering from disease and starvation that took place in the Nazi death camp at Dachau outside of Munich still hangs in the air there. One notices how close the camp was to residential houses. People living in the area had to have had an inkling of what went on inside the camp walls. There is no "good" way to write about Dachau. I chose to write in the voice of someone who lived in one of those houses. The Nazis operated Dachau longer than any other concentration camp. Some 206,206 prisoners were sent there, according to the regime's own records, and 31,951 people died there of starvation, exhaustion or unspeakable physical abuse. I wrote this poem to mark the 80th anniversary of the opening of the camp and read it at a program called "The News from Poems" in which each poem presented tried to make sense of something in the news. Still, there is no way to make sense of a place as monstrously evil as Dachau.

Litany

The throat of the world thirsts for blood.
Trigger finger itches for metal,
ear hungers for the rat-tat-tat of scatter shot.
No one is safe
—in a kindergarten coat room
—at an outdoor concert
—in a darkened movie theater
—at a Fourth of July parade
—in the produce aisle.
Heads explode like grapefruit,
spent rounds, like saw dust, on a supermarket floor.
There are bullet holes in skateboards,
brain tissue on the pages of history books.
School yards have become graveyards.
Lower your flags:
a nation stands accused.

For Reflection:

Gun violence is the leading cause of death among children and teens in the U.S. How then to write about such tragedy and do its victims justice? It is a rare poem that unleashes anger and does it well. Marie Howe, one of my early poetry mentors, would often say that arguments with others make for good rhetoric, arguments with ourselves make for good poems. I decided one way to write about the travesty of gun violence would be to state the facts in short declarative, unadorned sentences. In this way the poem becomes a prayer-like litany, albeit a litany of horror and tragedy.

English Mass, St. Boniface Church, Munich

The league of nations converges here
   in this *hausfrau* of a church basement:

wooden benches facing each other on either side of an aisle,
   altar in the middle covered with a plain white cotton cloth.

A Filipino man in a straw hat plays the guitar,
   a Nigerian passes out missalettes. The Vietnamese women

in the choir sing as though their lives depend on it
   and the Benedictine nuns from Kansas smile and nod.

It's Sunday morning, the English speakers' Mass
   at St. Boniface Church in this city named for monks.

Outside the Karlstrasse is dressed in baroque, a brass band plays,
   preparing for yet another summer street festival.

The priest from Cleveland steps onto the altar in brown Docker
   slip-ons, says we are all at times like David in 2 Samuel,

sending Uriah to his death at the front lines of the battle
   so David can bed Uriah's wife.

  Wanting what we want, wanting it now. And sometimes we are
   like the woman in Luke who washes Jesus' feet with her tears

while he forgives her sins. And isn't it just like Jesus to remind us
   that those forgiven the most are also the most willing to forgive?

The Filipino man removes his straw hat to sing the Lord's Prayer,
   croons with such conviction that I begin to weep.

I want to forgive everyone their trespasses, and to forgive my own.
    All the impatient judgments. The rushes of anger. The time

my inattentiveness made a friend cry. I want to bow my head,
    kneel, wash the feet of each person in the room with my tears.

For Reflection:

Sometimes an experience is just too rich, too overflowing with meaning to not write a poem about it. That is how I felt about the Sunday English Mass at St. Boniface Abbey Church which I attended on a brief visit to Munich. The palatable faith of the Filipino man who never took off his straw hat during the service except to sing *a cappella* The Lord's Prayer, the Vietnamese women in the choir, the Nigerian usher, the Benedictine sisters from Kansas, the celebrant from Cleveland in his flowing priestly robes and slip-on Docker shoes moved me to tears. So many times, when I attend a Catholic Mass anywhere in the world, the prayers, the songs, the surroundings feel so familiar, it is like a homecoming. What was surprising this time was how much these strangers seated in the pews beside me—people I would likely never see again—were able to teach me about myself.

At Thomas Merton's Hermitage on His Death Anniversary

There is something of mystery
   in the woodsmoke-scented air
      hugging this room where you embraced solitude,

kissed silence on both cheeks,
   slept in an impenetrable blackness
      that cupped you in its womb.

We've come to feel your presence,
   to salute the family of deer
      that lopes across the field beyond the sycamore,

to say to the doe as you would,
   I see you, sister. I know you.
      We run our fingers across the cedar desk

where you typed with two fingers,
   filled grid pages with infinitesimal handwriting,
     touching the desktop wood as if it too were a relic,

holy as the blackened Byzantine Mother and Child
   hanging in your chapel. The cinderblock walls
     vibrate with memories of your jazz LPs.

We imagine watching you through the bay window
   sway your body to Muddy Waters' *Got My Mojo Workin'*,
     to Wes Montgomery and Mary Lou Williams,

     as you tap your fingers along the imaginary bass strings,
        calling out, "Give it! Here! Take It!"
          Dancing with a work shirt swirling above your head.

When night descends, we watch lights blink on
   where Boone's farm used to be,
      let loose the intimations of an old self

like candle smoke rising. Vow to take more time,
   cover less ground, search for the inner sun:
      mercy within mercy within mercy.

For Reflection:

I have made many visits over the years to the Abbey of Gethsemani outside of Louisville where the great spirituality writer and Trappist monk Thomas Merton spent 27 years as a member of the monastic community. In the final three years of his life, he lived fulltime in a cinderblock hermitage in the woods a fair distance from the monastery. It is always a deeply moving experience for me to walk inside the hermitage's screen door. The spirit of Merton is still deeply present. In this poem, I pulled together pieces of what Merton had written in his personal journals and said on audio tapes about his life in the hermitage as I tried to imagine being there with him. Merton died on December 10, 1968 in Bangkok during a rare trip outside of his monastery and his small hermitage.

A Place Called Trouble

It springs from the ash heap of the afternoon news:
at last, a story that doesn't want to make you scream at God.

A story of This American Life
about a woman from San Francisco's China Beach

who wears head scarves and sports henna tattoos on her arms,
whose name, Giulietta Carrelli, sounds like poetry.

She opened a café she calls 'The Trouble'
to honor the people who helped her when she was 'in trouble'

which was most of her life. A place the size of a one-car garage,
formerly a front for cooking crystal methamphetamine,

that serves coffee, grapefruit juice, coconuts, toast and nothing
else. Coconuts halved and served with a straw and spoon

because that was the only food Giulietta could eat
that didn't taste like poison in her psycho-affective episodes

when she couldn't stand the sound of her own chewing
and because, people stop to talk when you're eating a coconut.

She's done a survey outside of her café, one day eating
an egg salad sandwich, the next a half-moon of coconut.

The grapefruit juice is for the Vitamin C. You can live
for months on just coconuts and grapefruit juice, Giulietta says.

She knows. She's tried it. And here's where the story
gets really interesting. The toast. Toast makes you feel safe,

"Nobody gets mad at toast."
I'm listening to this on the car radio in a conga line of traffic

driving home from Chicago to a town called Normal and a man I love
who has cooked a meal for me of fish, potatoes, green beans and bread.

Not toast, but a meal I imagine will taste like the entire menu
at The Trouble, spiced with a teaspoon of hope, a hint of second chances.

For Reflection:

Perhaps because I spent many years as a national journalist in both print and broadcast media, I often find material for my poems—not to mention quite a few spiritual lessons—in the day's news. National Public Radio offers a wealth of inspiration because of the often offbeat stories it tells. This one, which aired on "This American Life" had enough stranger-than-fiction elements, hidden life lessons, and eccentric wisdom to make it tailor-made for a poem. The lines come almost verbatim from the broadcast. The poem just about wrote itself.

Vine Growing Out of Stone Hermitage, Mount Maiella, Italy

for Jack Doyle

It springs from the limestone side
   of an ancient hermitage
      like a mottled face or a green heart
         set against a sea of gray stone

Emerald patch just large enough
   for a partridge to perch on
      it breaks through heart of rock
      finds its living water

Should a mountain goat amble above
   disturbing a tumbling rock,
      still it stares ahead
         fixed on the horizon

A single yellow flower
   rises from its chest
      dares to speak its name
         shouts what needs to grow will grow

will not be denied in this mountain vastness
   where wild winds rule
      gray wolf and red deer are companions
      and only beauty can save us

For Reflection:

Throughout Italy, there are substantial ancient buildings constructed out of seemingly impenetrable stone. Incredibly you will often see a vine, plant, or even a flower piercing through the stone. How in the world does such a seemingly fragile thing as a plant or flower get the strength to push through stone? How do they get the water and nourishment they need to survive, let alone thrive? These intrepid plants felt to me like the perfect metaphor to never underestimate the quest for life. They seemed to shout, what wants to grow will grow, no matter what. The mountain from which this hermitage is carved is a fascinating place where in almost Biblical fashion the red deer, gray wolf, and mountain goats co-exist. One feels both safe and awe-struck amid the mystery and natural beauty.

Summer of 2022

1.
The flags along Interstate 70 fly at half-staff,
lowered for the children and their teachers

at a school in Texas where the lunch bell
never rang that morning,

the vocabulary lesson still stares
silently from a chalkboard.

A friend writes: *I am so moved by the little girl
who played dead to save her own life.*

*What have we come to that we must
teach our children to do such a thing?*

2.
In a hospital room, a blinking monitor
measures my husband's pulse, the space

between his breaths, the lighted lines
rising and falling like mountain slopes.

Over a loudspeaker comes a Code Blue:
Room 13A. A heart stopped in mid-sentence, mid-breath.

Nurses awash in aquamarine scrubs rush past.
Later Brahm's Lullaby floats over the ward,

signals a baby's birth, proving song is stronger than death.

3.
We want to be sunflowers, always leaning toward the light
but the desert holds its hidden springs, secluded mysteries,

opens its dry mouth to the sun.

Some days I am the golden day lily, spreading my light,
other days shedding petals like minutes on a clock.

Some days I am my neighbor's collie, snout pointed
toward the wind, baying at the Sturgeon Moon.

4.
Across an ocean, war and more war.
Above the earth a telescope somersaults,

peers into remote reaches of the universe
like a god so far from the children in Texas,

from my husband, the day lilies, my neighbor's collie.
A god that perhaps too feels loneliness, terror in the night.

For Reflection:

Sometimes the tumult of our world syncs with the turmoil in our personal lives. When individual sorrow, like that which comes when someone we love is seriously ill, coincides with a public tragedy, like the school shooting in Uvalde, Texas, both experiences can feel deeply personal. We take sustenance where we find it, in a lullaby signaling a baby's birth, a collie watching the moon, a day lily springing up in a garden. Sometimes the only things that get us through the day are these small moments of grace and the intimation that somehow our sorrow is understood by a higher power, one that feels our fears, our loneliness, our sorrow.

What Peace Is

The charred shards of the houses
in Rafah move backward, reassemble,
stand erect again as in a movie rewinding

A tea kettle hisses on an iron stove,
steam curling from its spout, spreading mist.
There is milk in a porcelain pitcher, figs in a clay bowl

The open wound in the chest of a teenager
in Kharkiv closes over itself, its tender skin
healed again, replete with possibility.

His grandmother's scream returns to the throat,
her face relaxes into a smile,
clenched arms unfold into an embrace.

The *Birkot Hashachar* replaces a whispered *Kaddish*,
only cormorants pierce the sky,
and what flashes in the night are shooting stars

In quiet rooms, newborns feed on their mother's milk,
there are soft words, wool blankets,
IV lines turn into balloon strings

Stretchers lie empty as unmade beds,
olive groves grow tall in the desert,
streams run clear and cool

When we look into each other's eyes
we see our own reflection,
a tiny shrapnel of light, fragment of God

For Reflection:

Watching images of the brutal conflicts in Gaza and Ukraine and other war-shattered places cause us to feel powerless to help, to heal, to change a horrifyingly inhumane situation. Sometimes only a poem can speak about what is largely unspeakable. This poem imagines what it would be like to rewind the images that have become so sadly familiar. In this version of reality, the wounded are healed, babies are fed and cared for, and the dead come alive again. Perhaps it is an intimation of a hoped-for future when the killing stops, buildings are reconstructed, and life returns to some semblance of sanity. The poem gives voice to that hope.

PART III

Haibun for Point Reyes Peninsula

1.
The land here split apart
like a bone sundering
more than a century ago
in a tectonic civil war.

When plates beneath the earth grate one against the other and can no longer resist the strain, they fracture suddenly. Decades of accumulated energy pour out. The landscape trembles, changes within minutes.

Still the redwoods rise, peaceful watchmen,
some nearly as old as the dinosaurs.
They shoot hundreds of feet skyward
without tap root to anchor them,
while just-below-the-surface roots
spread shallow and wide
like dozens of interlocking arms,
a mystery of communion.

2.
Walking between cypresses,
madrones, bay trees and eucalyptuses,
I feel the stare of pairs
of hidden eyes: damselflies
secreted between branches,
bees building their sweet quarters
and ravens, plovers, bats,
quail, coyotes, deer and elk
coexisting in their own secluded condominiums.

Things eat each other and are eaten. Things fight each other for resources and cooperate for survival. Living things deplete and enrich the soil, are affected by and affect the local weather, are shaped by local topography and change it. Humans are part of this web of life.

3.
At Kehoe Beach, the sandstone cliffs
rest atop granite ridges
pushed up by earth's hot core.
Vincent cups a handful of sand,
looks up at me and says,
There are more galaxies
than these grains of sand in my hand.

If we could count five stars every second, it would take more than 10,000 years to count them all. Scientists estimate there are anywhere from 300 billion to 2 trillion galaxies. Considering that, 300 billion galaxies with 100 billion stars each gives us 30,000,000,000,000,000,000,000, or 30 followed by 21 zeroes worth of stars in the universe.

4.
Amid a field of shrub grass
lies a labyrinth of different colored stones
loosened from the soil.
It is the nameless handiwork
of some unknown women in town.
A stranger on the path hands me

an amber wildflower no bigger
than an infant's finger.
It is a perfect five-pointed star
with centered purple pistil.
I protect it from the wind
with my hand, itself a kind of star.

5.
There is a man from Inverness
they call The Planetwalker.
For 22 years he refused to use
motorized vehicles. He worried
about carbon dioxide in the air,
about oil spills in waters.
He walked in silence.
His footsteps were his words.

On his 27th birthday in 1973, John Francis decided as a gift to his community to stop speaking, to not argue for one day, and instead listen to what others had to say. He found this so valuable that he remained silent all of the next day. This continued, and he ended up not speaking for 17 years with the exception of a phone call to his mother after 10 years of silence.

6.
Mornings, a raven sends out
a single-note reveille,
exultant bugler,
urging the neighborhood
to delight in day.

Mist rolls in over Tomales Bay,
disappears by noon
as the sky clears to a fierce blue.

Sometimes the fog is so thick
at night along the coastline
even a mariner's keen eyes
cannot see the lighthouse beam
pulsing like a heartbeat,
beckoning travelers like a lovesick boy
longing for mystery, for touch.

For Reflection:

One of the greatest benefits of travel is that all of our senses are on high alert as we navigate unfamiliar territory. Point Reyes Peninsula in California, which includes the town of Inverness, boasts a multiplicity of tree species and an extensive list of creatures that make their home there. A poem seems to be lurking almost anywhere you look. The haibun form, which combines prose and poetry, seemed best suited to this place where the history, geography and true stories about its human inhabitants read stranger than fiction. This was in large part a "found" poem. Even the prose bits one reads about Point Reyes sound like poetry.

Anatomy

Have you saluted your heart today?
That tireless laborer, persistent percussionist
beating its bass drum as we work, eat, sleep, make love?

Have you placed your hand on your chest,
whispered to your heart as you would a lover?
Have you marveled at its hip-hop rhythm:

eighty beats a minute,
five thousand beats an hour,
forty-two million beats a year?

Have you stopped to praise your spleen,
fist-sized sorter of the essential from the extraneous,
the damaged from the intact?

Have you marveled at the pharynx and larynx,
conveyers of food, water and air,
at the tongue, that arbiter of taste,

or the glottis, sound engineer that allows us
to read aloud Dante's *Inferno, Goodnight, Moon,*
the 23rd Psalm? Have you considered

the beautiful regions of the brain:
the ganglia, the cerebellum, the parietal,
temporal and occipital lobes?

How they collaborate like NASA's mission control,
a hundred billion nerve centers
filling the eyes with Michelangelo's David,

the ears with Bach's Goldberg Variations,
moving the hands typing the words on this page,
directing my feet toward a cardinal perched on a lonely branch.

Have you not knelt in wonder at the sight
of a cell's inner workings, how it looks like a grid of Manhattan,
or set of archipelagos tossed in an ocean:

the mitochondria, the endoplasmic reticulum,
the Golgi apparatus, the membrane-bound organelles?
And why does this image of a cell make me think of Hayat Nazer,

a Lebanese artist who says she's never known peace,
who sculpted the figure of a standing woman
from bits of rubble, broken glass she collected after a Beirut blast?

A figure with wires for blowing hair, dress of scorched canvas,
a torch in her metal hand like the one the Statue of Liberty clasps,
her shrapnel face shouting of life beneath a defenseless, dusty sky.

For Reflection:

The Covid-19 pandemic set me thinking as never before about the human anatomy, how all these members fit together and work together in a form of machinery as complicated as a spaceship—except when they don't. Still, how can we not marvel at such connectedness, such craftsmanship? In the midst of the pandemic, some Harvard researchers released the most detailed image ever taken of a human cell, which itself is a model of watch-like precision. Add to that the unforgettable figure of a woman sculpted from the debris of war. It can never replace the real thing, and is itself a fusion of both human creativity and human folly. The Hayat Nazer sculpted woman and our flesh, blood and bone anatomy all seem of a piece to me, two visions of the human condition.

Chemotherapy

for Arturo and Nora Martinez

Dreams of *sandias* return to him now
from the dust of his Rio Grande past.
They taste of loam and the river,
melt like a communion wafer on the tongue.

Tamales too, pregnant with pulled pork,
sent to him from home in the Valley,
frozen into a brick, protected in foil,
and unwrapped like a gift on Christmas morning.

Lost now the desire even for these.

Mornings on the living room sofa
he plods through *The Times* crossword puzzle:
what is a five-letter word for Malignancy?
Six-letter word for Fix?

Samaritan chemicals journey through his veins,
take aim at the assassin in his gut
that holds a semi-automatic weapon,
its lock set on safety for one more day.

Late afternoon, his pregnant daughter brings
mango salsa, *calabacín tortitas* with their riot of onion,
cilantro, summer squash. Chips salted with memory.
He eats with his eyes.

Hungry bones consume his flesh.
Mañana waits behind the window shade.
When his daughter leaves saying, *See you tomorrow,*
they both believe it will be true.

For Reflection:

A poet-friend once told me of an uncle whose family knew he had terminal cancer and was expected to die soon. The family kept that information from the uncle and he lived several more years. As my friend said, "He didn't know he was supposed to die." What was it that kept my friend Arturo Martinez, to whom this poem is dedicated, alive through the long ordeal of chemotherapy and losing the taste for even the foods he loved most? I like to think it was the knowledge that his daughter would soon give birth to his first grandchild. When struggling, we need to hold on to that one thing that causes us to keep going, and if we're lucky, more than one thing.

Produce Aisle

Only a God with a sense of humor would invent the Brussel sprout:
miniature green skull concealed beneath cowls of green,

opening to dozens of tiny cells like the inner chambers of the brain,
tasting like life: sweetness and bitterness alike.

What are we to make of the rutabaga? Purple orb
like a Christmas ornament or punch ball,

growing wild on Swedish mountainsides as well as lowlands,
beloved of goats and cattle, food of last resort in two world wars.

And consider the practical joke of the onion. Whether clothed in
purple, aglow in amber, or awash in white, it will make you weep.

Whether it is raw, steamed, sauteed, pickled or fried,
still we cling to it as one would to a bad lover.

Who except one with an extravagant heart would invent
the humble parsley: never the main guest, always a plus-one?

Or the generous tomato? Faithful spouse of pasta and pizza,
traveling companion of salads and sandwiches,

progenitor of so many heirs: Roma, Early Girl,
Compari, Kumato, Big Beef, Brandywine.

What genius devised the pomegranate? A holy mystery,
the geographer Pausanias called it. A fruit older than Babylon,

its firm exterior opening to a cascade of ruby beads, sprung,
legend has it, from the blood of Adonis, enticing unsuspecting

Persephone to its forbidden cargo. Now think of the curlicues
of zucchini, wailing horns of eggplant, the celery's long mallets:

all in an immense palette of blooming colors more pleasing
than a painting. Who wouldn't stop, bow to this tableau of plenty,

observe a moment of silence, say thank you right there
in the produce aisle, and maybe even drop to one's knees?

For Reflection:

It always amazes me how plentiful produce is in this country. Because of our country's vast size and varied climates, we can have just about any fruit or vegetable on our table, whether they are in season or not. I love walking along the streets of European cities, and even the small grocery shops in New York City, where produce is displayed in neat, color-coded piles, as in a painting. In this ode to the produce aisle, I wanted to reflect on some of the more amazing fruits and vegetables. When I began to research different kinds of produce, I could see how each one has its back story, its unique narrative. Each one is its own small miracle. Who wouldn't bow down, and bend a knee?

To Joy

The hydrangeas' round white heads
    shout of joy, like the open faces of children.
Forget the sirens, shrieks in the street
    and exhaust of the traffic getting nowhere.
Let me tell you of the flamboyant cardinal
    skipping through ivy beside a slender sparrow
and the green hummingbird who hovers beside
    a window box of marigolds and impatiens
the way one might contemplate a still life
    by Cezanne.

From a far-off city a friend calls,
    barely able to speak, says dying is strenuous work,
asks me to remember that living is a dream job,
    like this morning when a shower
erupts on my walk, drenches my clothes with cool rain,
    sends up the sweet scent of wet grass.

Afterward a crack of light breaks through
    a floating bay of clouds and in no time
at all I'm warm again. Lately I have been thinking
    how the tiniest words brim with meaning,
settle in the mind, on the tongue when you least expect them.
    Words like *look, can, now, yes, joy.*

For Reflection:

There are times when the darkness and light of our lives arrive together, a package. The Japanese have a word for this: *komorebi*. It is formed from the words for tree, leak, and sun, and refers to those moments when sunlight "leaks" through leaves and branches, casting dark shadows on the ground. It is a reminder that we live within the constant tension of light and shadow. A phone call from a dying friend comes after a pleasant morning of watching the antics of birds. After a sudden rainfall, a streak of sunlight appears and we are warm and dry again. All is held in tension, but it is a beautiful tension if we view it as part of the privilege of being alive.

To Wonder

It doesn't have to be the green dust of a comet
streaking across the midnight sky
or the musical waves of a Bach concerto.

It can be these two feet, ten toes
gripping grass or loose sand,
eyes that glimpse a hummingbird tracing figure-eights,

fingers that clasp the soup spoon,
curl around the hand of the man I love
and a heart that drums without an orchestra,

simply for love. That there is dark bread, black tea,
mornings, and the moon's glitter across a rooftop
and not a missile's flash in the middle of the night.

That once a woman sheltered me in the cave of her body,
nourished me with her own blood. That a stranger
called to me in Osaka, led me to a side street

to see a cherry tree's umbrella of blossoms.
How I never forgot their velvet texture,
their version of pink, the kindness of that man.

How I learned to recognize the sound of my own name,
and the mockingbird's flute-like song, watched the light
of a 10-million-year-old star and shook stardust

from the surface of my own skin. How the sea
has a language all its own, and the crocuses return
each spring without prompting or persuasion.

How the hills turn from green to brown
to green again. The snow melts, the rains come,
and the sun reappears, faithful as a new lover.

That once in a cosmic lottery all the possible
jumbles of genes unlocked a singular combination,
a solitary ticket that leaves me breathless, lets me know I won.

For Reflection:

Some like to keep a gratitude journal. I like to keep a wonder journal. When you think about all the circumstances that had to fall into place for us to come into being, is it not a wonder that any of us come to be at all. That is the cosmic lottery we won by virtue of having been born. There are surely small moments of grace packed into every otherwise ordinary day. If you spend time each day looking for those wonder-filled moments, you will surely find them. Still, as a friend of mine who is a monk often reminds me, it takes effort and attention. As he puts it, "You have to be there."

The Almost, But Not Yet

for Carrie Newcomer

Shortened days. Still, they come carrying their breadbasket
of gifts, most of them unexpected, undeserved:

the green hummingbird buzzing like a bee above white petunias,
the raccoon hiding at dawn in the crook of a hickory tree. Already

I miss the praying mantis staring out from behind vinca vines,
the grasshoppers among the flowerbox geraniums, now moved on.

The crows begin their morning conversations later now.
Daylight grows paler. When I walk a dried leaf or two follows

me on the wind, scraping the sidewalk like an un-soled shoe.
This is the in-between time, the *almost, but not yet.*

Beside the back door a Swainson's thrush lies unmoving,
like some message launched from beyond. It probably

crashed into the glass at night. A body the size of my hand,
olive wings, black-striped breast, legs folded under, dark eyes

still as mirrors. I bury it next to a rose bush still blooming.
Few days remain to harvest, to glean, to walk barefoot

in the sacred grass or watch the bright bulb of Jupiter
dally with the cold light of the Harvest Moon. Time to set aside

jars of intentions for winter, to pull out final weeds,
to let go of what is broken, or piece it together again.

For Reflection:

Singer-songwriter Carrie Newcomer wrote a beautiful song called, "The Beautiful Not Yet" in which she describes those in-between times when one thing—a season, an experience, an effort—is starting to fade and something new is emerging. Living in the Midwest, spring often slips imperceptibly into summer without much contrast. Autumn, on the other hand, marks a clear break in the seasons, although there are days when it is hard to distinguish autumn from summer or from winter. Still, it is unmistakable that nature is winding down, preparing for its winter rest. The Swanson's thrush, lying dead outside the back door, is a harbinger of all that. At the same time, autumn is when we glean from the experiences that have gone before us in the past year, when we decide what we can let go of, what needs repair, and what we want to hold onto going forward.

River's Thaw

All through January
   we watched the river
      thicken and glaze

layer upon layer
    until its surface shone
       like a platform of quartz

though not even the deer
    dared test its strength,
       only some curious field mice,

an occasional pigeon
   or intrepid possum
      stitched tracks like an embroidered hem.

Below the surface the dark water roiled,
    churning the past year's recollections,
       the riddles of the coming spring.

By early March, rib cage cracks
    splintered the thick torso,
       needling their work in sunlight.

Sometimes in the night
    we would hear the ice groan,
       a woman straining in labor,

  awaken to a flotilla of diamonds
    each its own Iceland,
       each a disappearing territory.

Was it foolish to think what had seemed
    solid would never shatter,
        that a river could arm-wrestle time?

Slowly the water begins to breathe,
    releases the blue herring on their run.
        Spring peepers sound their chorus of bells,

a family of mallards
    skates figure eights
        on the water's hazy surface.

For Reflection:

I grew up in Bayonne, New Jersey, across from New York harbor on the other side of the Hudson River. One winter, a friend who still lives near where I was born clipped a photo that appeared in The New York Times of a massive layer of ice covering the Hudson. I had never seen the river so iced over. I began to imagine what was happening on the surface of that bed of ice and what was transpiring beneath it in the unseen waters. I thought about how inevitable it was that even this formidable layer of ice that had seemed so solid would soon break apart, groaning in the separation like a woman in labor. It drove home the impermanence of everything. The consolation: the coming of spring.

My Father's Down Vest

When I put on the olive-green vest
my father wore to ward off drafts, I become

someone who never exceeded the speed limit.
In 40 years of driving a Mack truck,

never had an accident, was philosophically
opposed to washing cars, saying, *That's what rain is for.*

I become someone who counseled his volatile daughter,
You catch more flies with honey,

that there are two things in life to remember:
when you're hungry you eat, when you're tired you sleep.

I become a man who never read Tennessee Williams
but clipped a photo from *The Daily News* of ice-covered trees,

titled it *The Glass Menagerie* and taped it to the basement wall.
The vest shines in worn spots, is still soft and plush,

enough emptiness there for the freedom of arms,
pockets large enough for a few coins, a handkerchief,

some peppermints, rubber bands. When I put on
my father's down vest, I become straight like an iris among nettles,

releasing a scent of peace, unscathed by surrounding thorns:
a singular bloom in an overgrown garden.

For Reflection:

My father was certainly a character, a "singular bloom." Someone who wrapped a red rubber band around his ring finger where other fathers wore their wedding band, who wore the same worn Navy-blue ball cap year after year. I don't know why, but when I was packing up some of his clothes to give away after his death, I couldn't part with the down vest that was as much a part of him as his ball cap and flannel shirts. I started wearing the vest around the house on particularly cold days. Putting it on brought back a flood of memories. I became my father. Perhaps everyone has a piece of clothing, an article of jewelry, a letter, an item of furniture, or something else that can evoke that kind of magical presence. My hope in writing the poem is that others will remember their own fathers, and see aspects of their fathers in mine.

Blessing

Every morning, I think about how bland
my world would be without dawn,

when the tongues of the lawn mowers have gone dumb,
replaced by the rising/falling hiss of the cicadas,

the dickcissel's whistle and the crows' repeating caws.
Or without the skunk who arrives at midnight,

leaves his gamey scent on the front doorstep,
like a calling card. To all this I say thank you.

And thanks to my dreadlock-sporting
newspaper deliverer Orlyn, a post-modern Elijah,

who arrives bearing *The New York Times*
so I can read about a spacecraft named Juno

hurtling toward Jupiter to pierce its inner core
and feel grateful I read *Bulfinch's Mythology*

in Sister Helen Jean's Latin class, can grasp the symbolism:
the jilted wife finally lancing her philandering husband's heart.

Soon there will be Bengal chai tea
with milk steamed in a silver pot from Siena,

a half-moon of grapefruit, some ten-grain bread,
dollop of I Can't Believe It's Not Butter,

and blueberry yogurt on the side.
I will look in the morning light at the face in the mirror,

the fine mouth lines, the brow crevice
that shout *Thank you!* for having lived this long.

Then who will judge me poorer,
drunk as I am on this cocktail of blessing?

For Reflection:

In one of her workshops, poet Marie Howe would encourage her students to take a difficult or traumatic experience they had endured and write a praise poem about it. This poem emerged at a time when two colleagues at the *NPR* station where I worked had died, and a beloved news director was retiring. To take the sting out of those events, I began enumerating the simple, quotidian items and events in my life that felt like blessings. When I began this list poem, the number of items kept getting longer. That is the thing about gratitude. The more you are grateful, the more you find to be grateful for. What would your list of blessings include?

About the Author

Judith Valente's chapbook *Inventing an Alphabet* was selected by Mary Oliver for the 2005 national Aldrich Poetry Prize. It was followed by her full-length collection, *Discovering Moons,* in 2009, published by Virtual Artists Collective/Chicago.

Along with Charles Reynard, Judith is co-editor of *Twenty Poems to Nourish Your Soul,* an anthology of poems and reflections. She is the author of five nonfiction books, including the memoir *Atchison Blue: A Search for Silence, a Spiritual Home and a Living Faith* and *How to Live*; and co-author of *How to Be* and *The Art of Pausing: Meditations for the Overworked and Overwhelmed,* a collection of haiku and short meditations.

Judith is a former staff writer for *The Wall Street Journal* and *The Washington Post* and on-air correspondent for national PBS-TV and two National Public Radio affiliates in Illinois. She was twice a finalist for the Pulitzer Prize in journalism and has won numerous awards for her journalism, poetry, and nonfiction writing. She is a sought-after speaker who frequently leads retreats on how to live a more contemplative life in the secular world and guides the annual "Benedictine Footprints" contemplative, cultural and culinary retreat/pilgrimage to lesser-known parts of Italy.

Website: judithvalente.com
Facebook: Judith Valente
Instagram: JudithValente_Author

www.ingramcontent.com/pod-product-compliance
Lightning Source LLC
Chambersburg PA
CBHW031202160426
43193CB00008B/470